MW01205851

EVANGELISM

Sharing the good news

By Roger K. Swanson
Updated by Shirley F. Clement
General Board of Discipleship

EVANGELISM

CONTENTS

Our Identity, Call, and Mission

Y ou are so important to the life of the Christian church! You have con-
sented to be among a great and long line of people who have shared
the faith and led others in the work of Jesus Christ. We have the
church only because over the millennia people like you have caught the
vision of God's kingdom and have claimed a place in the faith community
to extend God's love to others. You have been called and have committed
your unique passions, gifts, and abilities in a position of leadership, and
this guide will help you understand some of the elements of that ministry
and how it fits within the mission of your church and of The United
Methodist Church.

"The mission of the Church is to make disciples of Jesus Christ. Local
churches provide the most significant arena through which disciple-making
occurs" (*The Book of Discipline of The United Methodist Church, 2004,*
¶120). The church is not only local but also global, and it is for everyone.
Our church has an organizational structure through which we work, but it
is a living organism as well. Each person is called to ministry by virtue of
his or her baptism, and that ministry takes place in all aspects of daily life,
not just within the walls of the church. Our *Book of Discipline* describes
our mission to proclaim the gospel and to welcome people into the body of
Christ, to lead people to a commitment to God through Jesus Christ, to nurture them in Christian living by various means of grace, and to send them
into the world as agents of Jesus Christ (¶121). Thus, through you—and
many other Christians—this very relational mission continues. (The
Discipline explains the ministry of all Christians and the essence of servant
ministry and leadership in ¶¶125–137.)

Essential Leadership Functions

Five functions of leadership are essential to strengthen and support the ministry
of the church: identifying and supporting leaders as spiritual leaders, discovering current reality, naming shared vision, developing action plans, and monitor-
ing the journey. This Guideline will help you identify these elements and set a
course for ministry.

Lead in the Spirit

Each leader is a spiritual leader and has the opportunity to model spiritual
maturity and discipline. John Wesley referred to the disciplines that cultivate a
relationship with God as the "means of grace" and suggested several means:
prayer, Bible study, fasting, public and private worship, Christian conversation,
and acts of mercy. Local church leaders are strongly encouraged to identify
their own spiritual practices, cultivate new ones as they grow in their own
faith, and model and encourage these practices among their ministry team participants.

Discover Current Reality

"The way things are" is your current reality. How you organize, who does what, how bills get paid and plans get made are all building blocks of your current reality. Spend time with people who have been in this ministry and with your committee members to assess their view of how things are. Use "Christian conversation," one of the means of grace, not only to talk to others openly about their understanding of current reality but also to listen for the voice of God regarding your area of ministry.

Name Shared Vision

"The way things are" is only a prelude to "the way you want things to be." When the church is truly of God, it is the way God would envision it to be. Spend time with your committee and with other leaders in the church to discern the best and most faithful future you can imagine. How can you together identify your role and place in a faithful community that extends itself in its fourfold mission of reaching out and receiving people in the name of God, relating people to God, nurturing them in Christ and Christian living, and sending them forth as ministers into the world? Examine your committee's role and its place in that big picture and try to see yourselves as God's agents of grace and love.

Develop Action Plans

How do you get from here (your current reality) to there (your shared vision)? As a leader, one of your tasks is to hold in view both what is and what is hoped for so that you can build bridges to the future. These bridges are the interim goals and the action plans needed to accomplish the goals that will make your vision a reality. Remember that God may open up many (or different) avenues to that future, so be flexible and open to setting new goals and accepting new challenges. Action plans that describe how to meet interim goals should be specific, measurable, and attainable. While it is faithful to allow for the wondrous work of God in setting out bold plans, balance that boldness with realism. You and your committee will find information and tips here on developing and implementing the shared vision, the goals toward that vision, and the specific action plans that will accomplish the goals.

Monitor the Journey

A fifth responsibility of leaders is to keep an eye on how things are going. Setbacks will surely occur, but effective leaders keep moving toward their envisioned future. Not only will you monitor the progress of your committee's action plans to a faithful future but you will also be called to evaluate them in light of the ministry of the rest of the church. Immerse yourself and your plans in God's love and care. Voices from the congregation (both pro and con) may be the nudging of God to shift direction, rethink or plan, or move ahead boldly and without fear. Faithful leaders are attentive to the discernment of the congregation and to the heart of God in fulfilling the mission of the church.

Why Evangelism Is Important

You have been chosen to be a leader in your congregation, with responsibility for the ministry area of evangelism or witness. There is no more important work of the church than the task of reaching out to people with the good news of Jesus Christ and welcoming them with genuine Christian hospitality so that they may develop a relationship with God and live as Christian disciples.

Each of the Gospel writers, in his own way, describes how Jesus sent out his disciples to make other disciples for him. The best known is the Great Commission of Matthew 28:16-20:

> Now the eleven disciples went to Galilee, to the mountain to which Jesus had directed them. When they saw him, they worshiped him; but some doubted. And Jesus came and said to them, "All authority in heaven and on earth has been given to me. Go therefore and make disciples of all nations, baptizing them in the name of the Father and of the Son and of the Holy Spirit, and teaching them to obey everything that I have commanded you. And remember, I am with you always, to the end of the age."

(See also Mark 16:14-20; Luke 9:1-6; 24:44-49; John 20:19-23; Acts 1:6-8.)

Obeying the Great Commission is not one option among many for a congregation; it is at the very heart of the Christian enterprise. Christianity is a missionary, evangelizing faith. On the night of Jesus' birth, an angel described his birth to simple shepherds as bringing "good news of great joy for all the people" and sent them off to find the world's Savior "wrapped in bands of cloth and lying in a manger" (Luke 2:10, 12). The shepherds went to nearby Bethlehem, and finding Jesus and his mother and father, they "made known what had been told them about this child" (2:17). We can be sure that they later shared their discovery with their families and friends.

The first evangelist was an angel. Notice how the word *angel* (or messenger in Greek) shows up in the word *evANGELism*. That aside, the word *evangelism* is derived from Greek and literally is translated as "good message." In succeeding translations it became "gospel" and "good news."

What was the good news? It was Jesus himself. Jesus still is the good news that the creator God loves creation and acts toward it with grace and mercy. In Jesus Christ, God has come among us, identified with us, and continues to meet us in our deepest needs. The message is also what Jesus taught and preached. It was the good news of God's kingdom come and God's invitation for us to enter it and enjoy its benefits. Finally, the good news is what Jesus did. His death on the cross and God's raising him from the dead offer the peoples of the world forgiveness of sins and eternal life.

Good news always bears repeating. On the first Christmas Eve, the angel told the shepherds. They, in turn, told Mary and Joseph and certainly their families as well. And the story goes on. Those who heard Jesus teach told their friends how he spoke with authority. Those who were healed told "their" good news. Those who witnessed the resurrection of Jesus could not suppress the news, as astonishing as it was. The disciples soon became apostles on a mission of telling the good news throughout the world of their time. Consequently, from the day of Pentecost (Acts 2) onward, thousands of people were drawn into the church. Those people became evangelists or heralds, sharing their faith in Jesus and their experience of a new life in Christ.

Even persecution did not keep early Christians from telling the Christian story. In Acts 8:4 we find that it was not just the apostles who took the gospel out from Jerusalem but also those laypersons who were evicted from the city following the martyrdom of Stephen. In a word, if Jesus is who he says he is—the way, the truth, and the life (John 14:6)—then it follows that the work of evangelism, or witnessing, is central to Christianity and to each congregation of disciples.

Congregations gather for worship, learning, and fellowship. Congregations also scatter for witness and service, for telling and living out the good news of God's love for humankind and the world God has made. It is the rhythm of the gospel. Christians gather and scatter, gather and scatter. It is much like breathing. Breathing consists of inhaling and exhaling. Which is more important, breathing in or breathing out? It depends on what you did last, doesn't it? Wholeness in Christian experience requires the congregation gathered in community to worship and scatter throughout the community to serve! In fact, churches are unique in that they are the only groupings of people that exist not for members only but also for those who are not members, namely, the unchurched or disconnected.

Our own experiences as Christian disciples empower us to share the gospel with others. As we experience God's presence and power in our lives and as our faith grows stronger, we want to share that faith with others. Then our church becomes a place that welcomes, supports, and cares for our members and for our neighbors.

The Process of Making Disciples

As you begin to think about the focus of your work as a leader in evangelism ministries, think of your own experience of coming to faith in God. What role did a congregation play? For most of us, we would not be Christians were it not for a Christian congregation or congregations that reached out to us and welcomed us, inviting us to commit our lives to Christ and equipping and empowering us to live as Christian disciples. The truth is, it takes a congregation to make a disciple and to sustain a disciple in the Christian walk.

It takes a congregation to make a disciple.

Congregations make disciples not so much by holding events that welcome, invite, and support, but by developing a congregational lifestyle and an atmosphere, or environment, that is welcoming, inviting, encouraging, and empowering. A major factor that shapes congregational lifestyle and atmosphere is attentiveness to God and to the faith development of every person in the congregation. Other factors are trust, generational and ethnic inclusiveness, hospitality, a positive self-image, spiritual leaders—both lay and clergy—who embody and equip the congregation and its ministries, and a vision to serve the community beyond the cozy walls of the church building.

In many congregations, the work of evangelism has been limited to the upkeep of the church rolls and to sponsorship of an annual evangelism event. *Evangelism is, at its heart, sharing faith with others, particularly with those who are unchurched or disconnected, and inviting them to follow Jesus Christ as Christian disciples.* Congregations that are successful in carrying out the Great Commission of Jesus have developed a disciple-making system that begins with welcoming and invitation and continues through a process of relating persons to God and equipping and sending them forth in ministry. Congregations that are not receiving new persons on profession of their faith or that have a high percentage of inactive members are, in fact, getting the results that their evangelism plan (or its lack) is guaranteed to produce. A new plan or system is needed. This resource will help you as a spiritual leader to work with your pastor and others in developing a system that invites people to follow Jesus, forms them as disciples, and sends them out as Christ's agents.

Job Description

As leader of the evangelism ministry of your church, you have various responsibilities. These include:

1. Serving as team leader for those assigned to work with you, guiding the work of the team, helping them to work from a biblical and theological foundation, creating work space in which Christian faith formation happens, planning agendas, presiding at meetings, and representing the ministry of evangelism in meetings of the church council and charge conference.
2. Working with the pastor and team in assessing your congregation's vital statistics that relate to growth, such as membership (paying particular attention to professions of faith) and attendance trends as well as the way in which new people are received into the congregation and empowered for ministry.
3. Envisioning what God's will and dream for the congregation's future might be and setting goals that are consistent with that vision.
4. Developing a plan for an overall evangelism strategy and system that reaches out to persons, welcomes them into the congregation, relates them to God, and equips and empowers them for ministry.
5. Implementing your plan.

How to Get Started

1. Building the Evangelism Ministry Team
It is important to build a team of persons committed to the ministry of evangelism. A team differs from a committee in that a team is personally involved. Have you ever seen a committee play a game and win? A committee often is formed to be representative of a larger group. Committees can be contentious because of conflicting points of view of various parts of the larger body. *A team, on the other hand, is aligned around a single purpose.* Depending on the size of the congregation, a team should consist of no fewer than five and no more than a dozen persons. In other words, it should be a workable number. An evangelism team should be made up of persons who are already involved in evangelism ministries. Who are the welcomers and inviters in your congregation? They should be on the team. Include someone connected to youth ministry. Your team should represent a cross section of the congregation. However, do not include persons just because they might represent certain groups. *Personal commitment to the ministry of evangelism is vital.*

If you do not currently have an evangelism team, you might want to include as members your lay leader, any lay speakers in the congregation, and a youth. Start building your team with prayer. Pray for God to guide and empower your team. Evangelism is ultimately the work of the Holy Spirit. We can be effective servants and witnesses only as we nurture our personal relationship with God and seek God's guidance with others. At your first meeting determine a time of day when team members will be in prayer for one another and for the development of a common vision for the congregation's evangelistic ministry.

Agree on a reading schedule and include this Guideline on it. Ask your pastor to arrange for you to receive *The Interpreter,* the official program journal for United Methodist leaders. In addition, order some of the resources listed at the end of this Guideline. As team leader, you might want everyone to read the same resource, or you may want to divide up the resources among members of the team. You will find it helpful to set aside time at each team meeting for prayer and for a discussion of what each person is reading. (See *Staying Focused* in the Resource section for specific help.)

Read the Bible not only for your own spiritual formation but also for models related to evangelism and faith sharing. Important passages in this regard include:
● Matthew 9:35–10:23 (call and mission of the disciples)
● Luke 4:16-21 (Jesus' sermon in the synagogue)
● Luke 8:26-39 (Jesus expulsion of unclean spirits)
● Luke 10:1-20 (mission of the seventy)
● Luke 10: 25-37 (parable of the Good Samaritan)
● Luke 15 (parables of the lost sheep, coin, and son)
● John 1:35-51 (call of Jesus' first disciples)
● John 20:19-31 (post-resurrection appearance of Jesus).

Read the Book of Acts for a description of the missionary evangelism of the early church and the way that a vital church reaches out to new groups of people.

2. Assessing Current Reality

One of your first tasks ought to be to develop a sense of the strengths and weaknesses of the congregation. What is your church presently doing to reach out and welcome persons into the church's fellowship, to teach them, and to relate them to God? How effective are these activities? What are the results? You can measure these by assembling the reportable vital statistics of the last five to ten years: membership, worship and Sunday school attendance, and faithfulness in stewardship. If these data are not readily available, check the conference journal. The statistical pages include every church's membership growth, average worship size, and Sunday school attendance. *The most important statistics concern the number of people joining the church on profession of faith, the net growth or decline each year, and the average weekly attendance at worship, Sunday school, and other small groups.* Statistics related to giving can also be helpful to measure growth in discipleship. Is giving on the rise? What is the percentage of giving to mission projects in and through the local congregation?

Another important piece of information concerns the numbers of members who are considered inactive or marginal. Inactive or marginal members are embarrassments to most churches. There is also some degree of hostility toward them because they are not "pulling their weight." You must overcome reluctance to deal with this issue if you want to know the current reality in your congregation. So, name your inactive members. Who are they? Doing this will take some effort, but often a group of six to ten members, meeting together, can identify the level of involvement of each person in the congregation. The percentage of marginal members is a vital sign of the discipleship system currently in place.

Obtaining demographic data about your community is helpful. Your conference office may have such information for your community. If that office doesn't have it, you may contact the Office of Research of the General Board of Global Ministries directly, which can supply this information. (See the Resources section for details.) From these findings, you will be able to determine the numbers and age groupings of people in your community. Undertaking an outreach ministry to single persons would be a futile endeavor if there is not a significant number of single adults in your community.

When these data are assembled, spend enough meeting time to analyze the material prayerfully. What is God saying to you through it—"Well done, thou good and faithful servants," or "The harvest is plentiful, but the laborers are few"? How many persons have been received on profession of faith each year in the last five to ten years? In any given year in recent history, as many as half of United Methodist congregations have not received one person in this category. Yet more than any other, this category measures the success of the congregation in making new disciples. The percentage of inactive members is also a critical number. A higher percentage of inactive members points to an inadequate system for keeping members on the path to discipleship.

An important aspect of current reality that bears study is the climate of the congregation. Although it is difficult to define, a congregation's climate is the first impression made on visitors. Is the congregation friendly? Or is it self-centered? Are people glad to see one another? Are the people friendly only to their friends, or are visitors welcomed with genuine hospitality? Attitudes and relationships affect the climate. What are the attitudes in the congregation toward change, the future, and the growth of the church? You would be surprised at how quickly visitors overhear attitudes. How do people get along with one another? Remember the "new" commandment Jesus gave his disciples, "that you love one another." "By this," he continued, "everyone will know that you are my disciples, if you have love for one another" (John 13:34-35). Ask persons who have joined the church within the last six months to help you sense the climate of the congregation. These persons still have some objectivity left and can tell you what's right about the climate and what, if anything, was a barrier, which by joining the church they obviously overcame.

Various studies show that between 75 and 90 percent of new members affiliated with their present congregation because of a "relational factor." Check this out with your ad hoc team of new members. How did they make friendships? What is the congregation doing to encourage this development? Does the church have a coffee (tea, cocoa, cola) hour at a convenient time on Sunday mornings? Are visitors invited? To look at additional information, it may be helpful to contact persons who visited your congregation but did not continue. How did they perceive the climate of the congregation? What could the congregation be doing that would have been more helpful for them?

In reviewing all of this information, the team should strive for objectivity. You are seeking to learn whether or not you have a discipleship system in place that is working, not to assign credit or blame or to rationalize the data.

See "Our Church's Hospitality to Visitors" on page 23, and discover how friendly the church really is.

3. Developing a Shared Vision

"Few, if any, forces in human affairs," writes Peter Senge in *The Fifth Discipline,* "are as powerful as shared vision" ([New York: Doubleday/Currency, 1990], p. 206). Vision has been defined in different ways. It is the art of seeing the invisible, a visual image of a desirable future, hope with a blueprint. What we know is that vision is essential to growth, and a vision that is shared by a large number of people is already becoming actualized. In other words, a congregation's vision is where it is actually heading. The author has asked dozens of church members about the future of their church. On occasion, someone expresses a pessimistic view such as, "We probably won't have a church in five years." Often that vision comes true. On the other hand, a positive vision gives energy and direction.

A process for developing a shared vision among an evangelism ministry team should begin with prayer. People must be willing to let go of their pre-suppositions and personal agendas about what the church should be doing and center on discovering God's will and dream. They need to learn what God blesses—not set forth what they want God to bless—and then do that. People need to listen to one another as well. Spend time in team meetings on the personal vision or hopes that people have for their church. Who are the people left out or ignored in your community? What one thing could the church do that would make the most difference? Build a consensus. Is there one vision that the team is willing to embrace and recommend to the congregation? Be sure it is achievable. You don't want to waste energy on the impossible. Be sure, also, that everyone agrees on a goal. If people accept one vision as a compromise, without fully believing in it, there may be compliance but not commitment.

The vision must be shared with the church council and other teams in order for an integrated vision to develop, which will empower the congregation to move forward.

4. Establishing a Plan
It is common wisdom that when we fail to plan, we plan to fail! Remember that the mission of the church is to make disciples for Jesus Christ. Vital, growing congregations will have a comprehensive plan for evangelism—that is, a discipleship system in place that reaches out to people wherever they are, receives them as they are, relates them to God, nurtures them in discipleship, and sends them out as witnesses to the love of God in Jesus Christ. Your task is to lead the evangelism ministry team in designing your congregation's discipleship system. This is more important than planning evangelism events. If the discipleship system in your church does not result in professions of faith and a high level of involvement among your members then no evangelism event, no matter how well planned and executed, will be effective.

A discipleship system needs to focus on these areas: *welcoming, incorporating persons into the congregation,* and *equipping and sending them out as disciples of Jesus Christ.* The following pages will assist you and your team in developing a comprehensive plan for evangelism.

5. Setting Your Plan into Motion

Congregational inertia does not give way to plans. Action causes change to occur. Your whole discipleship plan does not need to be in place before you begin a part of it that your team believes is essential. If you have no greeters on Sunday morning, your team could take on that task as early as the next Sunday and keep on until a greeting ministry is more formally organized. Your team could choose to study personal faith sharing and could covenant to begin by each team member's filling out a F-R-A-N Plan (see "Implementing Your Evangelism Plan") and agreeing to be held accountable by the team.

As a team leader in evangelism, you would do well to remember two more things: keep cool, and have fun. Jesus' last words to the disciples on the Mount of Commissioning were, "And remember, I am with you always, to the end of the age" (Matthew 28:20). Christ is the head of the church and has promised his presence in all your efforts, step by step. God's work is not all work. There are friendships and deep satisfactions as we offer our best and creative efforts in the work of evangelism. Joy is one of the fruits of the Spirit (Galatians 5:22). As a friend likes to say it, if joy is missing in the work of evangelism, only the "news" section of the "good news" is present!

Implementing Your Evangelism Plan

Accccording to *The Book of Discipline of The United Methodist Church,* the mission of each church is "to make disciples of Jesus Christ" (¶120; see also ¶¶121-122). Congregations need not spend time in defining the church's mission. It is already stated. It is the primary task of the church in fulfilling that mission to:

reach out to people wherever they are and receive them as they are,
relate them to God through Jesus Christ,
nurture and equip them for Christian discipleship, and
send them out into the community to be the church in the family, the neighborhood, the community, and the world.

As you read, put a star by the ideas in the following categories you want to explore with your team and with the congregation.

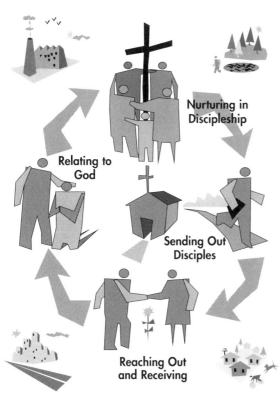

Nurturing in Discipleship

Relating to God

Sending Out Disciples

Reaching Out and Receiving

Turning Up the Thermostat

There is a difference between a thermometer and a thermostat. A thermometer registers the temperature; the thermostat changes it. The climate of a congregation is most affected by attitudes and relationships within the congregation. Attitudes and relationships, in turn, are affected mostly by the continual spiritual renewal of persons. My relationship with God most profoundly affects my attitudes and relationships. In other words, focus on the spiritual! Helping persons find a sense of the presence and grace of Christ in their lives and in the life of the congregation will do more than any particular program.

John Wesley promoted a personal and congregational lifestyle focused on what was called the means of grace—the "means," in other words, that lead to the sense of Christ's presence. *These "means" are prayer and fasting, Bible study, worship and the sacraments, Christian conversation, and acts of mercy.*

In pursuing such means of grace, vital congregations commonly do three things: *they promote (1) the small group experience, (2) a congregation-wide, focused Bible study, and (3) personal involvement in ministry and mission.*

You may want to consider offering small group experiences to your members. (See, for example, Covenant Discipleship groups in the Resources.) These groups are an adaptation of the early Methodist class meeting for the church of today. They are organized for the purpose of mutual support and accountability. Some churches offer Wesley groups for fellowship, prayer, and study. Remember that the Christian enterprise began with a small group experience of twelve persons.

Witness is a small group study that has been specifically designed to help individuals feel more comfortable and become better equipped to share faith and invite people into the body of Christ. A second part of the study helps change the climate and culture of the congregation to be one of "witness."

DISCIPLE Bible Study groups have also been found effective for changing the congregational climate. DISCIPLE Bible Study groups gain the benefits of the small group experience while also having the possibility of aligning a congregation around a sharply focused Bible study. There are many testimonies from churches that started to grow in evangelism outreach as they became more involved with DISCIPLE Bible Study. After all, the Bible is the best source of what the church needs to become.

Companions in Christ is yet one more small group experience in which persons may gain confidence in sharing their faith. Companions, over the course of twenty-four weeks, try out different methods of the means of grace, such as prayer and Bible study, mainly for devotional use. Through the *Companions* journey, participants grow in experience and in spiritual maturity, which is a key building block in faith development and discipleship.

Personal and congregational mission involvement is transformational. United Methodists support the mission of the church at large by meeting their apportionment obligations. But they meet their Lord when they go in mission to a neighbor in need or on a mission project in their own town or

hundreds of miles away. Few things raise the spiritual temperature of a congregation like the personal transformation and ownership of the church's mission resulting from personal involvement in mission and ministry.
See the Resources section for helps in small group ministries, *Witness,* DISCIPLE Bible study, *Companions in Christ,* and mission involvement.

Invitation and Welcome

A widely held perception in American culture is that church property is private property and that churches are for members only. To change this perception, congregations must become more intentional in invitation and welcome. To whom does your church send its newsletter? to members only? What does that say? Be sure to include recent visitors, families of church school children, and—if you can get their addresses—persons who attend community groups in your church. Consider the following possibilities.

The F-R-A-N Plan

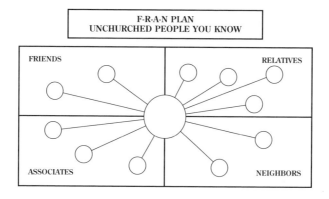

The F-R-A-N Plan is a part of the training in faith-sharing that can be established independently. Ask your members to list unchurched or disconnected friends (F), relatives (R), associates (A), and neighbors (N) who are not practicing Christians. Give them a diagram or the *Personal F-R-A-N Plan: A Ministry* leaflet available through Discipleship Resources. Ask your members' commitment to pray for these unchurched and disconnected friends each day and to invite them to church for worship or some other congregational event.

"I pray that the sharing of your faith may become effective when you perceive all the good that we may do for Christ" (Philemon 6).

Bring a Friend Sunday

Set one Sunday each month and ask your members to bring a friend. Have greeters at the door and design the worship experience so that visitors will feel welcome. Printing the Lord's Prayer and listing the number in the hymnal of the sung responses would help. Ask your pastor to preach something very basic on that Sunday to help visitors understand what United Methodist Christians believe. The goal is to get United Methodists to be invitational until every Sunday becomes "bring a friend Sunday." In the meantime many churches have found this a good beginning. Recruit other congregations in your community to go along with the project and do joint promotion in the local newspaper. Be especially aware of inviting others when "Igniting Ministries" media campaigns are done in your area. (These are sponsored through United Methodist Communications and your local area churches.)

Establishing Relationships

Faith-sharing is relational evangelism. Most people come to a relationship with God through Jesus Christ because of conversations and invitations from persons with whom they have relationships of trust. New relationships can be developed through tutoring or mentoring programs through the church. Individuals may establish relationships with people who are not connected to a church through fitness centers or through conversations with people at Little League games or other events they frequent. What are the kinds of non-intrusive random acts of kindness your congregation can offer?

Faith-Sharing Training

United Methodist members are often reluctant to share their faith with their friends and even with family members and are hesitant to invite them to church. They feel inadequate and uncertain. They want to know what is appropriate and what is not appropriate in sharing personal faith. United Methodists do not want to be intrusive or dogmatic. Resources are available for any local church to inaugurate training in personal faith sharing that is neither intrusive nor dogmatic. You may want to start a pilot project with a small group or with a youth or adult Sunday school class using materials in the Resources section. Or you may want to consider incorporating faith-sharing training in your new member orientation and in meetings of United Methodist Women and United Methodist Men.

Visit Your Visitors

It is a Christian courtesy for a congregation to respond promptly to a visitor's attendance at worship or some other congregational event. *Studies indicate that the sooner a response is made, the better the chances that the person will affiliate with the congregation. The same studies show that a visit by a layperson or a lay couple is most effective.* The best setting for such a response is a face-to-face meeting in the person's home or workplace. Consider the cultural expectations in your community. Some areas expect unannounced visits; others are repelled by them. If there is any doubt, call for an appointment before visiting.

You may choose to respond not only with a visit, but also with a small gift, perhaps a dessert for the family table or a loaf of home-baked bread. It would also be helpful to have a "leave-behind" information piece about the congregation with key telephone numbers and times for worship and Sunday school. If at all possible, have one or two church members ready to become mentors or guides and to establish a relationship with newcomers.

Tell Your Story

The best advertising is always word of mouth, but there are innovative ways of telling your story. Only members read the church page in the Saturday paper. Consider an ad in the real estate or obituary section. Or if you are starting a new ministry or service of worship, your young people may distribute leaflets by putting them under the windshield wipers on cars in supermarket parking lots on Saturday mornings. Direct mail can be effective as long as it is not overdone. Consider a mailing about the values of a Christian education to all the addresses in the zip codes of your ministry area when public school starts in August or September. Many churches have an artist in their membership who could design a Christmas postcard to be sent to all visitors in the past year who haven't affiliated. Easter is another time when people are more conscious of their spiritual needs.

Making Membership More Meaningful

Assimilating new people into the congregation needs to be a priority with the evangelism ministry team. Studies of congregational life reveal that as many as one-half of those who join churches become inactive in their first year of membership. This situation reveals a broken system of assimilation of new members. Remember that the mission is to make disciples, not members. The task is not complete, in other words, when people join the church. The issue in welcoming visitors is for them to feel like honored guests. The issue for people who actually join the church is for them to feel like members of the family.

When new members are graciously and intentionally assimilated, they
● continue to grow spiritually through small groups
● have at least seven personal friends in the congregation
● have identified gifts and callings and are exercising them

- understand, identify with, and support the mission and vision of the congregation
- are excited about the congregation and naturally invite friends, family members, and neighbors to become disciples of Christ.

To assist in this process, assign sponsors or fellowship friends to each new member person or family. These "shepherds" would help introduce new-comers to other congregation members and Sunday school class leaders and get them invitations to fellowship events.

Design and manage, under the pastor's direction, a plan whereby persons interested in exploring Christian faith or church membership could have opportunities to learn about Christianity, United Methodism, and the mission and ministry of your own congregation.

Assist newcomers in the congregation in identifying their own visions, gifts, and callings. Evidence exists that each person has to be connected to a congregation in three ways to stay connected: a worship connection, a fellowship connection, and a service connection. If newcomers can't attend worship, don't make any friends, or feel as if they are not needed, they will drift into inactivity.

Keep your eyes open! Maintain records to ensure that members are promptly missed and contacted if they begin to drift away. Register everyone's attendance at worship and Sunday school. In smaller congregations a sub-group of three or four persons could check the registration sheets each week and check off attendees. Retired persons could be recruited to make tele-phone calls from church in the daytime or from their homes at night. People feel important when they are missed! Studies of inactive people show that, in many cases, people will test out becoming inactive to see whether anyone will respond. One man, who had been absent from church for a few weeks, responded to a team from church, "I wondered if anyone would miss me."

Relating People to God
Your congregation's spiritual life is nurtured in a variety of settings: wor-ship, personal devotions, private and group study of the Bible, personal faith sharing, small groups for learning and practicing the spiritual disci-plines, and discovering and using spiritual gifts. *The goal is a personal rela-tionship with God through Jesus Christ.*

It is important for the ministry team to spend time at each meeting in inten-tional spiritual formation. Ministry area members might share their own experiences of being formed in Christ. Asking questions, "Who have been the two or three most spiritually influential persons in your life?" and

"What one circumstance has influenced you the most in your spiritual journey?" can be discussion starters. Faith, we say, is caught more than taught. Leaders need to be the most contagious! (See *Staying Focused:Building Ministry Teams for Christian Formation*, listed in the Resources section.)

You might consider having a spiritual life emphasis sometime in the "great fifty days" between Easter and Pentecost. If the Walk to Emmaus is active in your area, it can be a valuable resource for helping people relate to God. The same is true of the wealth of resources available through The Upper Room that encourage and facilitate spiritual formation. You might consider sponsoring and supporting a person to attend the Academy for Spiritual Formation, sponsored by The Upper Room.

Equipping People for Service

Jesus announced that he had come "not to be served but to serve" (Matthew 20:28) and that he has set us an example, "that you also should do as I have done" (John 13:15). A disciple of Jesus is, first of all, a servant who sees God most clearly in the needs of others and reaches out to meet those needs. Service is the heartbeat of discipleship. "As the Father has sent me, so I send you," says Jesus to the church today (John 20:21). Discipleship is being sent forth to serve with the gifts God gives for that purpose.

Disciples are sent forth into their homes, schools, workplaces, and communities at large. The possibilities of service are beyond counting in the ministry area of every congregation. What has this to do with evangelism? Doing acts of mercy is one of the ways we tell the Christian story. Being in ministry is an evangelical act; it testifies to the grace and love of God in action.

Your team can assist by working with your pastor and with other teams in helping people identify their gifts for ministry and service, as well as where God is calling you to work in a community. It may be a food bank, a Habitat for Humanity project, an after-school tutoring program, a Meals on Wheels program, or a prison ministry. Service is evangelism come full circle. You who have received Christ now offer him to others in word and deed.

Consider the possibility of assisting in the establishment of a new congregation. The most effective evangelism strategy is establishing new congregations. In our United Methodist connection, new church development is the responsibility of conferences and districts. Ask your district superintendent if there is a new church development planned in your area. Volunteers are always needed to help in community-wide surveys by visiting in neighborhoods or using the telephone. New churches need experienced Sunday school teachers to help them get started.

Examine Your Effectiveness

How can we know if we are being effective in our ministries? Bishop David J. Lawson (retired) suggests asking five questions:

1. Are persons growing in relationship to God through participating in our congregations? Are they freely yielding increasing portions of their life to the influence of Christ's teachings?

2. Are persons growing in their knowledge of Scripture, the wisdom of the Christian Movement, and the history of our church? Are they moving beyond an elementary level of understanding?

3. Are persons giving evidence of increased Christian commitment by the way they live?

4. Are persons growing in compassionate world citizenship, actively learning about and responding to needs of others, and finding practical ways to express membership in this global United Methodist Church?

5. Are persons viewing our congregations as supportive centers of excitement and joy? Are we inventing new approaches to worship and programming that are responsive to the needs of unchurched persons living within our assigned parishes? Are we discovering new ways of learning what these needs and interests are?

(David J. Lawson, in *Discipleship Dateline*, November 1993, General Board of Discipleship.)

Our Church's Hospitality to Visitors

(10 points for each Yes, except numbers 5 and 6)

1. Does the church have ample parking?   Yes ____ No ____

2. Is there a specific part of the parking lot designated for visitor parking?   Yes ____ No ____

3. Are there greeters in the parking lot?   Yes ____ No ____

4. Are there adequate signs directing visitors to parking, restrooms, nursery, the sanctuary, and Sunday school?   Yes ____ No ____

5. Do greeters: *(5 points each)*
   a. Offer a friendly welcome?   Yes ____ No ____
   b. Introduce visitors by name to the usher? Yes ____ No ____

6. Do ushers: *(2 points each)*
   a. Help visitors find a seat?   Yes ____ No ____
   b. Provide each visitor with a bulletin?   Yes ____ No ____
   c. Introduce visitors to other worshipers? Yes ____ No ____
   d. Give each visitor a visitor badge, ribbon, or cross?   Yes ____ No ____
   e. Help a visitor find the nursery (if needed)? Yes ____ No ____

7. Do the members wear nametags?   Yes ____ No ____

8. Are visitors given the opportunity to register their attendance (name, address, phone, and other information) on a registration pad? Yes ____ No ____

9. Is the congregation alert to give a friendly welcome to visitors?   Yes ____ No ____

10. Does the pastor welcome visitors during the worship service?
    (Deduct 5 points if visitors are asked to stand or raise their hand.)   Yes ____ No ____

11. Do members get the names of visitors and introduce them to other members?   Yes ____ No ____

12. Are visitors invited for coffee or other refreshments (before or after the service)? Yes ____ No ____

13. If you have a "coffee time," are there persons designated to spot new people and to introduce and involve them in conversation with other members?   Yes ____ No ____

14. Does someone offer to take each visitor on a tour of the church building?   Yes ____ No ____

15. Is every visitor invited to a Sunday school class?   Yes ____ No ____

16. Are visitors provided an opportunity to meet the pastor?   Yes ____ No ____

17. Does someone invite each visitor to be his or her guest or go with that person to a church function?   Yes ____ No ____

18. Are visitors invited to a membership orientation class   Yes ____ No ____

19. Does someone call on each visitor within forty-eight hours?   Yes ____ No ____

20. Is your Sunday school and small group system being used to train and equip members to "share faith," reach out to people, and welcome newcomers into the fellowship?   Yes ____ No ____

Key for Tabulation

(10 points for each question, except 5 and 6. Total your score!)

0–24   Church hostile toward visitors.
25–49   Tolerant (cool) toward visitors.
50–74   Visiting is permitted, but not encouraged.
75–99   Lukewarm toward visitors.
100–124   Visitors are casually prepared for.
125–149   Visiting is encouraged.
150–174   Visitors are important and prepared for.
175–200   Visitors are treated like honored guests and potential members and will know you want them as part of your fellowship.

"Our Church's Hospitality to Visitors," page 29 from *Evangelism Ministries Planning Handbook* by Suzanne Braden, Discipleship Resources 1987; questionnaire developed by Rick Kirchoff. Used with permission.

Resources

Resources in Faith-Sharing
The Faith-Sharing Initiative

- *The Faith-Sharing Initiative* is a strategy for training the church's laity in how to share their faith. It is most effective when sponsored by annual conferences and districts, but individual congregations may secure the material and initiate the training. Five resources support the training initiative.

- *Faith-Sharing: Dynamic Christian Witnessing by Invitation,* by H. Eddie Fox and George Morris (Nashville: Discipleship Resources, 1996 ISBN 0-88177-158-9). A revised and expanded edition. The text answers the fundamental questions of why, who, what, when, and how of personal witnessing.

- *The Faith-Sharing Congregation,* by Roger K. Swanson and Shirley F. Clement (Nashville: Discipleship Resources, 1996. ISBN 0-88177-153-8). A strategy for doing evangelism based on the quality of congregational life, which includes building a discipleship system, paying particular attention to ministries of hospitality, personal relationships, storytelling, the domestic church of the family, and the church family as the Body of Christ.

- *The Faith-Sharing New Testament and Psalms* (Nashville: Cokesbury, in cooperation with Thomas Nelson, Inc., 1994. ISBN 0-687-48651-1). An inexpensive translation of the New Revised Standard Version with personal helps for those wishing to be grounded in the Christian faith and to share gracefully that faith with others and lead them to Christian commitment.

- *Personal F.R.A.N. Plan* (Nashville: Discipleship Resources. ISBN 0-88177-259-3). Sold in groups of one hundred. These wallet-size leaflets are designed for praying and for sharing one's faith with a friend, relative, associate, or neighbor.

- *Faith-Sharing Video Kit* (Nashville: Discipleship Resources, 1996. ISBN 0-88177-207-0).This video presents a six-session study of personal faith sharing, based on the book *Faith-Sharing*. A Leader's Guide is included.

- *10 FAQs of New Christians,* by Peter Harrington (Nashville: Discipleship Resources, 2000. ISBN 0-88177-304-2). Presents responses to the ten most often asked questions by seekers and new Christians. Available in English, Spanish and Korean.

For more information, contact Faith-Sharing Initiative Office, General Board of Discipleship, P.O. Box 340003, Nashville, TN 37203-0003.

Sharing Faith in the Family

• *FaithHome Leader's Kit* (Nashville: Abingdon Press, 1997. ISBN 0-678-06610-7). A nine-week church-sponsored experience in which families learn how to talk to God and how to talk to one another about God and faith.

Sharing Faith

• *Witness: Workbook and Journal Set,* by Ronald K. Crandall (Nashville: Discipleship Resources, 2001. ISBN 0-88177-322-0). *Witness: Video* (ISBN 0-88177-354-9). A 25-week small group study focused on exploring and sharing your Christian faith.

Invitational Preaching

• *Beyond the Worship Wars,* by Thomas G. Long (The Alban Institute, 2001. ISBN 1-56699-240-0).

• *Preaching to Head and Heart,* by Thomas R. Swears (Nashville: Abingdon Press, 2000. ISBN 0-687-06830-4).

Other Resources

• *A New Kind of Christian: A Tale of Two Friends on a Spiritual Journey*, by Brian D. McLaren. (San Francisco: Jossey-Bass, 2001. 078795599x).

• *Accountable Discipleship*, by Steven W. Manskar (Nashville: Discipleship Resources, 2000. ISBN 0-88177-339-5). Fundamental resource for persons involved in Accountable Discipleship ministries.

• *Beginnings: An Introduction to Christian Faith,* by Andy Langford, Mark Ralls, and Rob Weber (Nashville: Cokesbury, 2003), is a small group experience for adults hungry for an intentional walk with God that encourages a personal relationship with Jesus Christ. It is designed to begin where these adults are on their spiritual journey. *Planning Kit* (includes one of each: Director's Manual, Small-Group Leader's Guide, Participant's Guide, *Along the Way: A Participant's Companion,* set of videos/DVDs) (ISBN 0-687-06280-2). For more information contact Curric-U-Phone at 1-800-251-8591 or curricu-phone@cokesbury.com.

• *The Child Friendly Church,* by Boyce A. Bowdon (Nashville: Abingdon Press, 1999. ISBN 0-687-07574-2). Based on a study of 150 congregations, it is a guidebook for congregations wishing to reach out to children and to receive them with hospitality.

• *Christian Believer* is a thirty-week high-commitment study of the central teachings of the Christian faith. For information about training seminars call 1-800-251-8591; (fax) 615-749-6049; www.umph.com/christianbeliever.

- *Creating a Church Home: Preparing Adults for United Methodist Membership* (Nashville: Abingdon Press, 1997. ISBN X784173). Helps adults find their new church home in your local church. A three-ring binder includes the "Fellowship Friends" booklet (a guide for mentoring new members), "Multiply God's Love," "A Dictionary for United Methodists," and plans for nine sessions.

- DISCIPLE Bible Study, available in four phases, is a program of committed Bible study for small groups meeting each week. Contact: Cokesbury Seminars, 201 8th Ave. South, PO Box 801, Nashville, TN 37202; 615-749-6068; 300-251-8591; (fax) 615-799-6049. www.cokesbury.com/services/disciple.asp

- *Leading Beyond the Walls: Developing Congregations with a Heart for the Unchurched*, by Adam Hamilton (Nashville: Abingdon Press, 2002. ISBN 0-687-06415-5).

- *The Next Christendom: The Coming of Global Christianity,* by Philip Jenkins (New York: Oxford University Press, 2002. ISBN 0-195-14616-6).

- *Radical Outreach,* by George G. Hunter III (Nashville: Abingdon Press, 2003. ISBN 0-687-07441-X).

- *Staying Focused: Building Ministry Teams for Christian Formation,* by M. Anne Burnette Hook and Shirley F. Clement (Nashville: Discipleship Resources, 2002. ISBN 0-88177-295-X). Invites church leaders in committees and ministry areas to incorporate Wesleyan means of grace into their work. Specific suggestions are given for worship, stewardship, education, evangelism, and outreach.

- *Waking to God's Dream: Spiritual Leadership and Church Renewal,* by Dick Wills (Nashville: Abingdon Press, 1999. ISBN 0-687-00482-9). A testimony to the transformation that turned one church upside down (but right side up), changing its direction from declining to growing. This book will inspire and challenge readers to "go and do likewise."

- *What Every Leader Needs to Know* series (Nashville: Discipleship Resources, 2004).

- *Demographic data of your church and community* are available through the Office of Research, General Board of Global Ministries, 475 Riverside Drive, New York, NY 10115. Call 212-870-3840. Web site address: http://research.gbgm-umc.org/.

Resources in Spanish

- *El compromiso de compartir nuestra fe,* Manual del Participante, available from the Faith-Sharing Initiative Office, General Board of Discipleship.

- *La Congregación que comparte su fe: Un modelo para la congregación como evangelista,* by Roger K. Swanson and Shirley F. Clement; translated and adapted by José A. Malavé García (Nashville: Discipleship Recources, 2001. ISBN 0-88177-312-3).

- *Las 10 preguntas más frecuentes entre los nuevos cristianos,* by Peter Harrington, translated by Martha E. Rovira-Raber (Nashville: Discipleship Resources, 2001. ISBN 0-88177-330-1).

- *Manual Compartiendo la Fe* by Ramírez, Martínez, de la Rosa, Zambrano (Nashville: Discipleship Resources, 1996. ISBN 0-88177-185-6).

- *Manual de Evangelismo* by Ordáz, Volverde, Sevilla, Borbón (Nashville: Discipleship Resources, 1997) (ISBN 0-88177-185-4)

- *El Nuevo Testamento Y Salmos para compartir la Fe* (Nashville: United Methodist Publishing House, 2002). Available from: World Methodist Evangelism, 1008 19th Avenue South, Nashville, TN 37212-2166.

- *El Plan Personal de Alcance: un ministerio,* translated and adapted by Lía Icaza-Willetts (Nashville: Discipleship Resources, 2001. ISBN 0-88177-358-1).

Affiliate Organizations

- ***National Association of United Methodist Evangelists.*** This association includes in its membership the ordained elders who are appointed as general evangelists by their respective annual conferences, as well as lay or clergy people who work in other evangelistic ministries full or part time. For more information, or a recommendation for an evangelist, contact Charles Whittle at P.O. Box 24241, Fort Worth, TX 76124. Phone: 817-451-4408 Fax: 817-451-4409; e-mail: charleswhittle@juno.com.

- ***Foundation for Evangelism.*** Contact Paul Ervin, 551 Lakeshore Drive, Lake Junaluska, NC 28745. Phone: 800-737-8333, 828-456-4312. e-mail: paulervin@prodigy.net.

- ***Council on Evangelism.*** Contact: Dr. Gary W. Exman, 485 Cherrybottom Road, Gahanna, OH 43230. Office: 614/471-0252; Home: 614-471-7553. Fax: 614-471-0210. e-mail: gjexman@prodigy.net.

Spiritual Formation

Resources for spiritual formation are available through The Upper Room, P.O. Box 340004, Nashville, TN 37203-0004. Publications include:

- *Alive Now,* a bimonthly devotional magazine that supports the spiritual life of small groups as well as individuals.

- *Companions in Christ* series, includes *Companions in Christ: A Small Group Experience in Spiritual Formation* (available also in Spanish); *Companions in Christ: The Way of Blessedness; Companions in Christ: The Way of Forgiveness; Companions in Christ: The Way of Grace.* Each resource in the series includes a participant's book, Leader guide, and journal. Available through The Upper Room, 1-800-972-0433 or www.upperroom.org/bookstore.

- *Devotional books.* Each year The Upper Room publishes approximately twenty-five books that encourage and support the spiritual formation of Christian disciples. Write for a free catalog or access the Web site at http://www.upperroom.org.

- *Devo'Zine* is a bimonthly magazine designed to strengthen the spiritual life of teenagers. *The Devo'Zine Guide for Mentors and Small Groups* is a companion piece, published simultaneously with *Devo'Zine.*

- *Pockets* is a monthly devotional magazine to help children grow in their relationship with God.

- *The Upper Room Daily Devotional Guide,* published bimonthly, helps people listen to God. It is published in sixty-three editions and forty-three languages around the world, including the very popular *El Aposento Alto,* published in Spanish. The English edition is available in large print and on audiocassette. The daily devotional is also available via e-mail or on-line at http://www.upperroom.org/devotional.

- *Weavings* is a journal for spiritual leaders in the church, clergy and laity, who wish to deepen their spiritual lives.

On the Internet

Many resources for evangelism are available on the Internet. Here are some addresses:

- The Academy for Spiritual Formation www.upperroom.org/academy/
- "Ask Julian" (attempts to answer some of the questions of modern-day seekers.) www.upperroom.org/askjulian/
- Chrysalis ("Emmaus" experience of spiritual formation for teens and young adults) www.upperroom.org/chrysalis/
- Evangelism: www.gbod.org./evangelism/
- The Foundation for Evangelism: www.evangelize.org
- Igniting Ministries www.ignitingministry.org

- Leadership for Evangelism in the local church:
www.umc.org/churchleadership/layministry/witness/evangelism.htm

- MethodX (an online community for young adults to explore their relationships with God, with each other, and with the world around them.)
www.methodx.net

- The Walk to Emmaus www.upperroom.org/emmaus/

- Witness: www.gbod.org/witness

Also Recommended

- *Net Results* is a monthly magazine devoted to congregational vitality. Subscription information is available by writing to *Net Results*, 5001 Avenue N, Lubbock, TX 79412-2993. Telephone: 806-762-8094. e-mail: netresults@llano.net.

For additional resources, check with your annual conference office.